Sharing your Faith Without Fear

A 4-week course to help teenagers discover how they can share their faith in everyday circumstances

by Stephen Parolini

Loveland, Colorado

Group®

Sharing Your Faith Without Fear
Copyright © 1994 Group Publishing, Inc.

First Printing

All rights reserved. No part of this book may be reproduced in any manner whatsoever without written permission from the publisher, except where noted on handouts and in the case of brief quotations embodied in critical articles and reviews. For information write Permissions, Group Publishing, Inc., Dept. BK, Box 481, Loveland, CO 80539.

Credits
Edited by Michael Warden
Cover designed by Liz Howe and Amy Bryant
Illustrations by Rosalie Lawrence

ISBN 1-55945-409-1
Printed in the United States of America

CONTENTS

INTRODUCTION 4

Sharing Your Faith Without Fear

COURSE OBJECTIVES 4
THIS COURSE AT A GLANCE 5
HOW TO USE THIS COURSE 5
PUBLICITY PAGE 8

Lesson 1 — 9

What Do I Believe, Anyway?
Teenagers will explore the basics of their faith and create a faith-sharing journal.

Lesson 2 — 19

But What Do I Say?
Teenagers will express to others what it means to be a Christian.

Lesson 3 — 27

Everyday Faith
Teenagers will discover the powerful witness of living out their faith in everyday situations.

Lesson 4 — 34

Putting the Pieces Together
Teenagers will create a mobile illustrating what they've learned about sharing their faith.

Bonus Ideas — 42

Introduction
SHARING YOUR FAITH WITHOUT FEAR

"Go and make disciples of all the nations..."

Jesus left us with an awesome responsibility. But too often, today's young people don't believe Jesus' command is for them. They understand the need to share the good news but believe that's just for pastors, missionaries, and other Christian leaders.

But Jesus' command isn't directed solely at church leaders; it's directed at each Christian, no matter how young. In 1 Timothy 4:12, Paul reminds us that people of all ages can make a difference in building God's kingdom.

"But where do I start? What do I say?"

Many teenagers don't know where to begin when sharing their faith. Some mistakenly believe they must be great orators. Others expect they'll have to be brash, bold, and borderline obnoxious to get people's attention. And many are simply afraid of failure or rejection.

But teenagers don't have to spend years in seminary to learn how to share the good news. After brushing up on the basics of faith, today's young people can be extremely effective "everyday evangelists."

This course will help teenagers explore what they believe so they can become grounded in their own faith. It will give kids the confidence to talk to friends about their relationship with Christ. And it will help them discover the powerful witness they can have through their actions and everyday lifestyle.

Then, to help kids (and the whole church) remember the importance of sharing their faith with the world, teenagers will create a lasting symbol of what it means to share Jesus with others.

Help kids overcome their fears and shyness about telling the good news. Use this course to boost kids' confidence and energize the whole church to become everyday evangelists.

COURSE OBJECTIVES

By the end of this course, your students will
- learn the importance of knowing what they believe,
- create a faith-sharing journal,
- talk with others about what it means to be a Christian,
- show love toward people in the church or surrounding community,

- build a mobile symbolizing the faith-sharing experience, and
- commit to share their faith with others.

THIS COURSE AT A GLANCE

Before you dive into the lessons, familiarize yourself with each lesson aim. Then read the Scripture passages.
- Study them as a background to the lessons.
- Use them as a basis for your personal devotions.
- Think about how they relate to kids' circumstances today.

Lesson 1: WHAT DO I BELIEVE, ANYWAY?
Lesson Aim: Teenagers will explore the basics of their faith and create a faith-sharing journal.
Bible Basis: 1 Corinthians 15:1-11.

Lesson 2: BUT WHAT DO I SAY?
Lesson Aim: Teenagers will express to others what it means to be a Christian.
Bible Basis: Acts 17:22-34.

Lesson 3: EVERYDAY FAITH
Lesson Aim: Teenagers will discover the powerful witness of living out their faith in everyday situations.
Bible Basis: 1 Timothy 4:6-16 and Titus 2:1-8.

Lesson 4: PUTTING THE PIECES TOGETHER
Lesson Aim: Teenagers will create a mobile illustrating what they've learned about sharing their faith.
Bible Basis: Matthew 28:18-20.

HOW TO USE THIS COURSE

PROJECTS WITH A PURPOSE™ for Youth Ministry

Think back on an important lesson you've learned in life. Did you learn it by reading about it? from hearing a lecture about it?
Chances are, the most important lessons you've learned came from something you experienced. That's what active learning is—learning by doing. And active learning is a key element in

Group's new Projects With a Purpose™ for Youth Ministry courses.

Active learning leads students in doing things that help them understand important principles, messages, and ideas. It's a discovery process that helps kids internalize what they learn.

Research about active learning indicates that maximum learning results when students are involved in direct, purposeful experiences. With that in mind, each Projects With a Purpose for Youth Ministry course gives teachers tools to facilitate some sort of project that results in direct, purposeful experiences for teenagers. Projects, experiences, and immersion into real-life faith action characterize this curriculum. In fact, you could probably call this the "project" curriculum, since each course produces a tangible result. You'll find plenty of helpful hints that'll make this course easy for you to teach and meaningful to your students.

Projects With a Purpose for Youth Ministry takes learning to a new level—giving teenagers an opportunity to discover something significant about their faith. And kids learn the important skills of working together, sharing one another's troubles, and supporting one another in love.

Projects With a Purpose for Youth Ministry offers a fun, alternative way for teenagers to put their faith into action. Use it today to involve your kids in Christian growth experiences they'll remember for a lifetime.

Before the 4-Week Course

- Read the Introduction, the Course Objectives, and This Course at a Glance.
- Determine when you'll use this course. Projects With a Purpose for Youth Ministry works well in Sunday school classes, midweek meetings, home Bible studies, confirmation classes, youth groups, special-interest groups, leadership groups, retreats, camps, or any time you want to help teenagers discover more about their faith.
- Decide how you'll publicize the course using the clip art on the Publicity Page (p. 8). Prepare fliers, newsletter articles, and posters as needed.
- Look at the Bonus Ideas (p. 42) and decide which ones you'll use.

Before Each Lesson

Read the opening statements, Objectives, and Bible Basis for the lesson. The Bible Basis focuses on a key biblical theme for the activity, experience, or Bible study portion of the lesson.

Gather necessary supplies from This Lesson at a Glance.

Read each section of the lesson. Adjust as necessary for your class size and meeting room.

Helpful Hints

- The approximate minutes listed give you an idea of how

long each activity will take. Each lesson in a Projects With a Purpose for Youth Ministry course is designed to take about an hour. Some lessons may require work outside of class, depending on the project for the course. You might also consider restructuring your class time, if possible, to allow more time to complete projects.

> The answers given after discussion questions are responses your students *might* give. They aren't the only answers or the "right" answers. If needed, use them to spark discussion. Kids won't always say what you wish they'd say. That's why some of the responses given are negative or controversial. If someone responds negatively, don't be shocked. Accept the person and use the opportunity to explore other angles of the issue.

■ If you see you're going to have extra time, do an activity or two from the "If You Still Have Time..." section at the end of each lesson or from the Bonus Ideas (p. 42).

■ Dive into the activities with the kids. Don't be a spectator. The experience will be more successful and rewarding for both you and your students when you play an active role.

■ Have fun with the lessons as you lead your teenagers. Remember, it is Jesus who encourages us to become "like little children." Besides, how often do your kids get *permission* to express their childlike qualities?

■ Be prepared for surprises. In Projects With a Purpose for Youth Ministry lessons, you don't always know which way the lesson will go. Much of your job will be directing kids to stay on task rather than leading specific activities. As facilitator, you'll be helping kids make their own faith discoveries rather than directing the results of a specific activity.

■ Encourage new leaders to participate in teaching this course. Projects With a Purpose for Youth Ministry offers an exciting way to give new volunteers a hands-on look at the positive impact youth ministry can have on teenagers.

■ Rely on the Holy Spirit to help you. Remember, only God can give true spiritual insight. Concentrate on your role as the facilitator and trust the Holy Spirit to work in the hearts of your kids.

You Can Do It!

Because Projects With a Purpose for Youth Ministry is a different approach to Christian education, leading the lessons might seem a bit scary at first.

That's OK. In fact, it's normal to be a little nervous about a new teaching method. Innovation often requires a risk for the teacher. But hang in there. With the Holy Spirit's guidance and your own desire to make these lessons succeed, great things will happen in your kids' lives.

PUBLICITY PAGE

Grab your teenagers' attention! Photocopy this page, then cut out and paste the clip art of your choice in your church bulletin or newsletter to advertise this course on sharing your faith. Or photocopy and use the ready-made flier as a bulletin insert. Permission to photocopy this clip art is granted for local church use.

Splash the clip art on posters, fliers, or even postcards! Just add the vital details: the date and time the course begins and where you'll meet.

It's that simple.

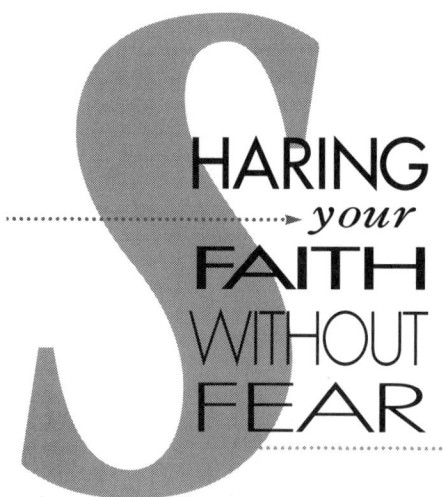

A 4-week experience to help you learn practical ways to share your faith with others

Come to ....
On ....
At ....

Come examine what you believe—and how to share your beliefs with your friends.

What Do I Believe, Anyway?

LESSON 1

Have you ever had someone try to explain something to you that he or she obviously didn't understand to begin with? Pretty embarrassing, isn't it? Well, the same is true with our faith. Before we tell someone about Jesus, we need to know what we believe. This lesson will help kids explore the foundations of the Christian faith.

Teenagers will explore the basics of their faith and create a faith-sharing journal.

Students will
- learn the importance of knowing what they believe,
- explore what they believe about faith basics, and
- create a faith-sharing journal.

Look up the following key Bible passage. Then read the background paragraphs to see how the passage relates to your teenagers. This Scripture will be explored during the Bible study portion of this lesson.

In **1 Corinthians 15:1-11**, Paul defines the importance of the Resurrection.

In these few verses, Paul sums up the main issues regarding our Christian faith. Paul emphasizes Jesus' post-Resurrection appearances to the disciples and others to focus on the fact that Jesus is indeed still alive today. He reminds his readers that if Christ had not risen from the grave they would believe in vain.

Paul, having once been a zealous persecutor of Christians, worked hard to bring God's message of love to his world. In verses 9 and 10, he introduces another important faith issue when he explains that he worked hard to grow in faith, yet it was God's grace that brought him this far.

These verses point out the most significant issues Christians must understand before they can tell others about Christ. First,

LESSON AIM

OBJECTIVES

BIBLE BASIS

1 CORINTHIANS 15:1-11

we must embrace the truth that Jesus died for our sins, was buried, and rose again. Second, we must know that God's grace is a gift—we can't win it by doing good works. This is a significant point for teenagers in today's performance-based society. Finally, we can learn from Paul's example that we must give our all to grow closer to God and do God's work.

With these basic beliefs as a foundation, we can begin to unravel the mysteries of faith through studying the Scripture. And teenagers who feel uncomfortable with their faith can grab on to the basics and move forward with confidence, sharing Jesus' love with others.

THIS LESSON AT A GLANCE

Section	Minutes	What Students Will Do	Supplies
Introduction	up to 10	**Sharing Your Faith**—Define the purpose of this course and introduce themselves in a creative way.	
Bible Study	up to 10	**Know-It-Alls**—Attempt to explain difficult concepts to each other.	Bibles
Project Work	up to 30	**What Do I Believe?**—Work in small groups to explore faith basics and create faith-sharing journals based on their discoveries.	Newsprint, markers, small notebooks, pencils, "Faith-Sharing Journal" handouts (p. 16)
	up to 15	**Commitment**—Determine how they'll share their faith in the coming week.	"Our Commitment—Week One" handouts (p. 17), pencils
Closing	up to 5	**Help Me to Know**—Ask God to give them wisdom about sharing their faith.	

The Lesson

INTRODUCTION

Sharing Your Faith
(up to 10 minutes)

Welcome students to the class. Say: **Today, we're going to begin a four-week course on sharing our faith. We're going to explore practical ways to live out Christ's command to bring the good news to the whole world.**

During the next four weeks, we'll explore what we believe about basic faith issues, practice talking with others about our faith, experience what it means to live out our faith, and share what we've learned with the whole church.

Open with prayer.

Say: **Since we'll be working closely together for the next few weeks, let's begin our course by getting to know each other a little better.**

Form groups of no more than four. Have kids each tell their partners one hobby or activity they really enjoy. Then have students work together in their groups to come up with a pose or action to represent each person's hobby or activity.

Allow no more than four minutes for groups to come up with their poses or actions. Then have one group stand in front of the class and perform each pose or action for the rest of the class. Ask class members to first guess what the actions represent, then match up which person(s) from that group enjoys that hobby or activity.

Continue until each group has had a chance to act out its hobbies or activities.

Say: **Just as each person here has unique interests and hobbies, we each have a different way of sharing our faith. In the coming weeks, we'll explore a variety of ways to share our faith. But before we can tell anyone what it means to be a Christian, we need to understand what Christians believe.**

Know-It-Alls

(up to 10 minutes)

Form groups of no more than four. Assign each person in the group one of the topics from the "Terms" box in the margin. Then say: **Beginning with the person who has the term "scion," explain to your group members what the word means. If you don't know, do your best to explain what you think it means. The goal is to have your group members understand the term's meaning. When I call "time," move clockwise around your group and have the next person define his or her term.**

Give each person 30 seconds to explain his or her term to the group. Call time when appropriate to allow the next person to speak.

After teenagers have explained their terms, ask the following questions. Allow time for small-group discussion, then ask volunteers to share their groups' answers.

■ **What was it like to explain something you didn't fully understand?** (Frustrating; difficult; I didn't know what to say.)

■ **What did you feel as you tried to understand what someone was explaining?** (I felt embarrassed; I was completely lost.)

■ **How is this experience like or unlike your experience of telling someone what it means to be a Christian?** (I don't explain my faith very well; I think my faith is easier to explain.)

Have volunteers take turns reading aloud a few verses of 1 Corinthians 15:1-11 until the entire passage is read. Say: **These verses describe key issues we must understand before we can tell others about Christ. In this passage, Paul explains that Christ died for our sins, was buried, and rose again.** Then he

BIBLE STUDY

Terms

Assign the following terms to teenagers. Don't let them know the actual definition until after the activity.

• mercerize (to treat thread to strengthen it and make it slightly glossy)

• ossify (to change into bone, or to make or become set or rigid)

• quiescent (at rest or inactive)

• scion (a shoot or branch used for grafting, or a young descendent of a family)

LESSON ONE ■ 11

PROJECT WORK

goes on to say that ==God's grace is a gift==—we can't win it by doing good works. Finally, we discover from Paul's example that we must give our all to grow closer to God and do God's work.

Ask:

■ **Why is it important that we know the basics of faith when telling someone about Christ?** (We must be confident to share our faith with others; we can't explain why we're Christians unless we know what Christianity is all about.)

Say: **With so many different churches, religions, and belief systems, it can be difficult to sift through and find what's most important about the Christian faith. And while it's true that we may never fully understand all the facets of faith, we can begin to struggle through the issues to find out what the foundation of faith really includes.**

What Do I Believe?

(up to 30 minutes)

Have kids form groups of no more than four. Photocopy and cut apart the "Important Issues" handout (p. 15). Then give one topic to each group from those listed on the handout. Tape three sheets of newsprint around the room and mark each with one of the following headings: "Critical," "Not Critical," and "Unsure." Give each group a different color marker.

Say: **In your group, discuss the topic you've been assigned and determine whether you believe the truth of this statement is absolutely critical for Christian faith. If you believe it is critical, write that statement on the "Critical" newsprint. If you believe the statement, however important, isn't absolutely critical to the faith, list it on the "Not Critical" newsprint. If you really can't decide, write it on the "Unsure" newsprint.**

After you've made your decision and written the statement on the appropriate newsprint, come to me and get another statement to work on.

See how many statements you can get through in no more than 10 minutes. Then have kids discuss the following questions:

■ **Do you agree with the other groups' decisions? Why or why not?** Answers will vary.

■ **What does this activity tell us about the issues that are most important to our faith?** (The basics are most important; the important issues are things most Christians truly believe.)

■ **What role do items listed on the "Not Critical" newsprint play in dividing Christians?** (People who believe that these noncritical issues are critical tend to leave when others disagree.)

■ **What does this activity tell us about the role faith plays in Christianity?** (We must trust God about things we don't understand; if we don't have faith, we can't tell others what it means to be a Christian.)

■ **How can we use this knowledge when telling someone about our faith?** (We can avoid talking about things that aren't critical; we can share the truth simply.)

Have kids find partners. Ask partners to decide who will be the "extrovert" and who will be the "introvert." Then say: **So far, we've been exploring the "intellectual" side of our faith. We've looked at the theologies that are important to our faith. But the personal, real-world part of our faith is often the most powerful expression of our faith to others. Beginning with the extrovert, tell your partner what it means to you to be a Christian. Focus on what's different in your everyday life. For example, how are your actions different? How are the words you use different? Why are you a Christian?**

After two minutes, call time and have the introverts explain what it means for them to be Christians. Then, after another two minutes, ask:

■ **How do your personality and experiences affect the way you tell others about Christ?** (I speak from experience; I speak with passion about faith issues.)

Give kids each a pocket-sized notebook, a photocopy of the "Faith-Sharing Journal" handout (p. 16), and a pencil.

Have kids follow the instructions on the handout and complete their first entries in their notebooks. Allow about five minutes for kids to complete their entries, then say: **Hang on to your journals because we'll be adding to them each week. You may also write in them during the week, if you wish. Then in the fourth week, we'll use all the notes in our journals to create a mobile that represents what it means to share our faith.**

Commitment

(up to 15 minutes)

Form pairs. Give pairs each a photocopy of the "Our Commitment—Week One" handout (p. 17) and a pencil. Say: **To continue your exploration of what it means to be a Christian, determine one thing from this handout you and your partner will do during the coming week. The key to making this handout work is to choose something you know you and your partner can do successfully.**

Read the ideas, then choose the one you'll do. Hold your partners accountable by calling them once or twice during the week. Or, if possible, meet during the week to follow through on your plan together.

When pairs have determined what they'll do to further explore what it means to be a Christian, have them checkmark that item on the handout, then sign it. Make a photocopy of each pair's handout and save it until next week's class.

Say: **Next week, we'll begin the class by reporting on how our commitment plans worked and what we learned from them. Then we'll practice sharing our faith by talking with younger children about faith.**

Teacher Tip

Be aware that arguments may break out among group members as they discuss these issues. If that happens, allow the discussions to continue until they seem to be "going nowhere," then use that teachable moment as a way to help kids understand the conflicts that often occur between Christians over these issues. For example, you could ask, "How are your reactions like the reactions different churches sometimes have toward each other? What's the best way to resolve these conflicts without building walls between ourselves and other Christians?"

LESSON ONE ■ 13

CLOSING

Table Talk

The "Table Talk" activity in this course helps teenagers explore with their parents what it means to share their faith with others. If you choose to use the "Table Talk" activity, this is a good time to show students the "Table Talk" handout (p. 18). Ask them to spend time with their parents completing it.

Before kids leave, give them each the "Table Talk" handout to take home or tell them you'll be sending it to their parents. Tell kids to be prepared to report next week on their experiences with the handout.

Help Me to Know
(up to 5 minutes)

Have pairs from the previous activity merge to form foursomes, then have groups stand in small circles. Say: **This week we've taken the first step in learning how to share our faith better. But we can't do any of this without the support of friends or without God's help. Let's close in silent prayer, thanking God for each other and asking God to help us know what to say when telling someone about Christ. I'll close in a moment with an "amen."**

Ask kids to hold hands or put their arms around each other as they pray. After a moment of silent prayer, close with an "amen." Then remind students to follow through on their commitment plans in the coming week. Encourage kids to take their journals home and record any insights from their experiences.

Next week, you'll be matching up teenagers and younger children for discussions about what it means to be a Christian. You might want to talk today with kindergarten through fifth-grade teachers to make arrangements for the activity. Look on page 22 for a description of the interaction between teenagers and the younger kids.

If You Still Have Time...

What Do Others Think?—Send kids out to interview other church members about the issues they think are most critical to Christian faith. Then have kids report their discoveries in next week's class.

Familiar Verse—Form groups of no more than four and have groups read John 3:16 and discuss why this verse is so often used in sharing Christ with others. Ask kids to compare their "Critical" statements from the "What Do I Believe?" activity to the message of this verse.

IMPORTANT ISSUES

Directions: Photocopy and cut apart the topics on this handout for use during the "What Do I Believe?" activity.

- Jesus is God's Son.

- The Bible is the perfect Word of God.

- Jonah was swallowed by a large fish.

- If you are truly a Christian, your actions will give evidence of your faith.

- Jesus walked on water.

- Jesus died on the cross.

- You can find the answers to all of life's problems in the Bible.

- Jesus rose from the dead.

- Jesus brought Lazarus back to life.

- We were created to live in relationship with God.

- God flooded the whole world, and only Noah's family and the animals were spared.

- Not all "good" people will go to heaven.

- The end of the world will come exactly as it's described in Revelation.

- Love is the most important ingredient in Christian faith.

- Studying the Bible and participating in church are the most important ways Christians grow closer to God.

Permission to photocopy this handout granted for local church use. Copyright © Group Publishing, Inc., Box 481, Loveland, CO 80539.

FAITH-SHARING JOURNAL

Your faith-sharing journal will be a record of your discoveries during this four-week course. Use the following ideas to get your journal started.

1. Write your name on your journal.

2. On the first page, write two or three sentences describing how you felt when you learned the topic of this four-week course.

3. List the issues you believe are the foundation of Christian faith based on what you've discussed about statements written on the "Critical," "Not Critical," and "Unsure" newsprint sheets.

4. Think of a friend who you don't think is a Christian. Then list three reasons you wish he or she would become a Christian.

5. Choose a partner and exchange journals. Write on the inside of the front or back cover one thing you appreciate about your partner and how that thing relates to the topic of sharing your faith. For example, you might write, "I like the way you listen to others. I think that will be a great benefit when non-Christians ask you questions about what it means to be a Christian."

6. Retrieve your journal and hang on to it. You'll need it each week.

Permission to photocopy this handout granted for local church use. Copyright © Group Publishing, Inc., Box 481, Loveland, CO 80539.

OUR COMMITMENT—WEEK ONE

Sharing your faith is something that usually happens outside of church. Use one of the ideas listed below to further explore what you believe and what it means to be a Christian. Call your partner during the week to keep each other accountable to the task you've chosen. We'll discuss this experience next week.

Commitment Ideas:

❑ Contact four non-Christian friends and ask (in a caring and sensitive way) why they aren't Christians. Record their answers in your faith-sharing journals. (If they want to talk more about faith, use this opportunity to tell what you believe.)

❑ Go to your local library, find a book about various religions, and see if you can determine what makes Christianity unique.

❑ Invite two Christian friends to join you for a discussion about what scares you most about telling friends about Christ. Brainstorm ways you can overcome your fears.

❑ Read Philippians 3:7–4:1 and discuss how this passage compares with your understanding about Christianity.

We, the undersigned, do hereby commit to follow through on the commitment plan checkmarked above.

Name_____ Phone _____

Name_____ Phone _____

Permission to photocopy this handout granted for local church use. Copyright © Group Publishing, Inc., Box 481, Loveland, CO 80539.

Table Talk

To the Parent: We're involved in a four-week course at church called Sharing Your Faith Without Fear. Students are exploring what it means to be a Christian and how to share their faith with others. We'd like you and your teenager to explore this important topic together. Use this "Table Talk" page to help you do that.

Parent

- What "turns you off" most about the way people share their beliefs with others?
- If you've ever told someone about what it means to be a Christian, what did you say? How did the person respond to what you said?
- Who or what has had the greatest impact on your faith?

Teenager

- What is the toughest thing about telling someone about Christ?
- What about Christianity do you wish you knew better?
- How might your non-Christian friends react if you told them about your faith?

Parent and teenager

- How can your lives show others what it means to be a Christian?
- What are specific ways you can develop your ability to share your faith?
- How can you help each other become confident in sharing your faith?

Read John 3:16, then paraphrase it as if you're telling a school friend or work associate about Jesus.
- Why is it sometimes difficult to let others know about our faith?
- Why is it important to avoid "religious" language when explaining what it means to be a Christian?

Pray together, asking God for the strength to tell others about Christ. Then make commitments to share your faith with one or two specific people. Think about how you'll express your faith—through words, actions, and prayers. Talk at least twice this week about how your commitments are going.

Permission to photocopy this handout granted for local church use. Copyright © Group Publishing, Inc., Box 481, Loveland, CO 80539.

But What Do I Say?

LESSON 2

Even when kids feel confident in their own faith, it's not always easy to tell someone about Jesus. Out of their desire to say the right thing, young people often confuse their audience by speaking in hard-to-understand religious terms. When kids learn to share their faith using everyday language, their friends can begin to really understand what it means to be a Christian.

Teenagers will express to others what it means to be a Christian.

Students will
- discover the importance of speaking about faith in simple language,
- talk with others about what it means to be a Christian,
- complete entries in their faith-sharing journals, and
- make a commitment to discover more about telling friends about Christ.

Look up the following key Bible passage. Then read the background paragraphs to see how the passage relates to your teenagers. This Scripture will be explored during the Bible study portion of this lesson.

In **Acts 17:22-34,** Paul preaches the good news in Athens.

Paul's message in this passage is directed to a group of nonbelievers, instead of to his more typical Jewish audience. Instead of teaching about God's fulfilled prophesies, Paul focuses his message on the providence of a *known* God (in stark contrast to the belief that an "unknown god" watched over Athens, the Greek center of culture).

Paul knew that the people really needed to discover the known God. So he spoke to them on their own level—fully aware of what they believed and clearly explaining the providence of God in terms they could understand. This is an important model for Christians to follow today. Instead of talking in "Christianese," we need to reach out to others where they are and speak their language.

It's appropriate to notice that not everyone listened to Paul

LESSON AIM

OBJECTIVES

BIBLE BASIS

ACTS 17:22-34

LESSON TWO ■ 19

and chose to follow God. Some even laughed. Once again, this is an important lesson for today's young Christians. Teenagers who are willing to speak out about their faith are eventually going to be ridiculed or ignored by at least some of their audience (perhaps a large majority). Yet by speaking clearly and from their own experience of faith, teenagers can open the door to Christ for their friends.

THIS LESSON AT A GLANCE

Section	Minutes	What Students Will Do	Supplies
Introduction	up to 10	**Nonsense Words**—Create nonsense words to describe themselves.	"Our Commitment—Week One" handouts (p. 17) from last week
Bible Study	up to 10	**Speaking Clearly**—Explore the importance of simplifying their language when talking about faith.	Bibles, paper, pencils
Project Work	up to 35	**Tell Me Again . . .**—Share basic faith concepts with younger children.	"Something to Talk About" handouts (p. 25)
	up to 10	**Commitment**—Determine how they'll share their faith in the coming week.	"Our Commitment—Week Two" handouts (p. 26), pencils
Closing	up to 5	**Simple Thanks**—Thank God for his guidance in their day-to-day evangelism.	

BEFORE YOU BEGIN...

The Lesson

During this week's class, you'll be matching up teenagers with younger children to talk about what it means to be a Christian. Talk with teachers of kindergarten through fifth-grade classes and arrange to have your teenagers meet with the children for about 20 minutes during class.

INTRODUCTION

Nonsense Words
(up to 10 minutes)

Welcome students to the class. Say: **Today, in our second week of this course on sharing your faith, we're going to explore the importance of speaking in clear and simple language when talking about what it means to be a Christian.**
Open with prayer.

Welcome visitors and class members who weren't here last week. Have a volunteer explain what the class is up to during this course.

Say: **Before we begin today's class, let's have commitment pairs share insights from their activities during the past week.**

Have kids find their partners from last week's "Commitment" activity. Distribute photocopies of the "Our Commitment—Week One" handouts (p. 17) pairs filled in last week. Have volunteers tell the whole class what they learned from their experiences. Encourage volunteers to share what was easy or difficult about following through with their commitments.

Thank kids for following through with their commitments.

Say: **Before we dive into today's Bible study, let's spend a few minutes discovering more about each other.**

Form groups of no more than four. Have kids each make up a "nonsense word" and attach a personal meaning to it that describes them in some way. For example, someone who likes to ski might come up with the word "shuttlefuzz" and determine it means "someone who likes to ski." Ask kids to tell their group members their descriptive nonsense words (but not the hidden meanings). Then have group members attempt to determine the hidden meaning of each person's descriptive nonsense word.

Allow a few minutes for discussion, then have each person explain the meaning of his or her nonsense word.

Ask:

■ **What was it like to guess the meaning of these nonsense words?** (It was impossible; it was kind of fun; I had no idea what to guess.)

■ **How might this be like the way people who aren't Christians feel when we use Christian terms such as "sin" and "grace" when talking to them about Christian faith?** (They're confused, too; it's the same because they don't have a clue what the words really mean.)

Say: **Today, we're going to experience what it's like to simplify the language of faith. Let's begin by exploring how Paul did this when speaking to non-Christians.**

Teacher Tip

In the event that some pairs didn't do their work during the week, ask what kept them from completing the task. For example, kids may say that busyness or an unexpected event caused them to not do their task. Without placing blame or judgment on those pairs, ask, "How is your situation like what happens in real life when we try to share our faith? How can we keep 'urgent' or 'pressing' things from squeezing out 'important' things like sharing our faith with others?"

Table Talk Follow-Up

If you sent the "Table Talk" handout (p. 18) to parents last week, discuss students' reactions to the activity. Ask volunteers to share what they learned from the discussion with their parents.

LESSON TWO ■ 21

BIBLE STUDY

Speaking Clearly
(up to 10 minutes)

Form groups of no more than four. Have kids each choose one of the following roles in their group: reader (who reads the Scripture passage), mumbler (who mumbles what he or she thinks the passage is about), interpreter (who attempts to interpret the mumbler's words), and recorder (who records the interpreter's insights).

Give recorders in each group a sheet of paper and a pencil. Have readers read aloud Acts 17:22-34. Then have the mumblers explain how this passage illustrates the importance of talking with non-Christians in their own language. Encourage mumblers to speak as incoherently as possible.

After a few minutes of mumbling, have the interpreters tell the recorders what they think their mumblers said. Finally, have recorders write what the interpreters told them, then read it to the whole group.

Then ask:
■ **How is what we heard from the mumblers like what non-Christians might hear when we tell them about being a Christian?** (They don't understand; it's difficult to know what we're saying.)

Say: **When we share our faith with non-Christians, they often just hear mumbling. But when we speak, as Paul did, in the language and culture of the people, others can get a glimpse of what it means to be a Christian. Thankfully, our words aren't alone in reaching out to others—the Holy Spirit guides our words and can reach into others' hearts even when we don't say the right things.**

Have groups again discuss the passage, but have everyone speak clearly this time.

Then ask the following questions, allowing time for discussion before having volunteers share their groups' insights:
■ **What was Paul's message to the people in Athens?** (God is a known God; serve God instead of false idols.)
■ **How did Paul reach the people on their level?** (He spoke about their unknown god and told them about the known God; he understood what they believed.)
■ **How can we share what it means to be a Christian to people who don't understand Christianity?** (Speak about things they do understand, such as hope; learn what their needs are and help them see how faith can fill those needs.)

Say: **For the next 20 to 30 minutes, you'll get to experience what it's like to talk about faith in simple language. We're going to talk with children about what it means to be a Christian.**

PROJECT WORK

Tell Me Again...
(up to 35 minutes)

Have teenagers pair up and give each pair a photocopy of the "Something to Talk About" handout (p. 25). Say: **Read the**

22 ■ LESSON TWO

instructions on this handout and take a couple of minutes to discuss how you'll proceed in your talk with the younger children.

After a couple of minutes, send pairs off to meet with younger children in the church. Have pairs each meet with two or three children. To assure a variety of experiences, assign a different class or age group to each pair (doubling up as necessary).

Give students about 20 minutes to talk with the children about what it means to be a Christian. Then have pairs return to class. Have teenagers take no more than four minutes to write in their faith-sharing journals any insights they discovered from their experiences. Don't let students talk about their experiences until everyone has made an entry into his or her journal.

Then have pairs get together to form foursomes. Have groups discuss the following questions. After discussion time, have volunteers share their groups' ideas with the whole class.

Ask:
■ **What was it like to tell someone about your faith?** (Exciting; uncomfortable.)
■ **How easy or difficult was it to explain Christian faith in simple terms?** (It was easier than I thought; I couldn't find the right words to say.)
■ **What surprised you most about this experience?** (These kids knew a lot already; it wasn't easy expressing my faith; I was able to speak in simple language.)
■ **What kinds of questions did kids ask? How did you respond?**
■ **What can you take away from this experience that will help you reach out to non-Christians in everyday life?** (I'll listen more and do less talking; I'll try to talk about how faith in God can change their lives.)

Say: **When we share our faith with others, not everyone is going to listen. Some will probably laugh, as Paul experienced in Acts 17:22-34. But our efforts are worth the ridicule.**

Commitment
(up to 10 minutes)

Have kids choose different partners for this week's "Commitment" activity. Then distribute the "Our Commitment—Week Two" handout (p. 26) and a pencil to each pair.

Have pairs read and complete the commitment handouts. Then have partners summarize today's lesson and write those summaries in their faith-sharing journals.

Say: **Next week we'll begin the class by reporting how our commitment plans worked and what we learned from them. Then we'll discover the powerful witness of living out our faith.**

Teacher Tip

If you're meeting during a time when no other classes meet, arrange to have younger children from your church or community attend this lesson. Or have pairs visit the children's classes when they do meet.

CLOSING

Simple Thanks

(up to 5 minutes)

For today's closing, form trios and have kids each take a turn saying a simple prayer of thanks for God's guidance in their day-to-day evangelism and for both the children they met and the person on their right. Encourage students to be specific as they pray and to speak their prayers in simple language.

After kids have prayed, remind them to follow through on their commitment plans in the coming week. Encourage kids to take their journals home and record any insights from their experiences.

Then say: **So far we've been exploring how to express our faith in words. Next week we'll express our faith through our actions. You'll want to dress appropriately next week because we'll be "getting our hands dirty."**

If You Still Have Time...

Alien Cultures—Have kids explore how they'd tell people from other cultures about Jesus. Encourage kids to brainstorm nonverbal messages they could give about God's love. Then have kids perform those messages and see if others can understand them.

Changing the Lyrics—Form groups of no more than three and give each group a church hymnal or songbook. Have kids search the songs for lyrics that don't fit today's culture and rewrite them in today's language. Have groups present their new songs to the whole class. Then sing one or two of the songs.

SOMETHING TO TALK ABOUT

When you meet with your group of children, consider the following format for your time together. As you go through these steps, be sensitive to the age level of the children you're speaking with. Keep your explanations simple and short.

1. Have each person (including you) introduce himself or herself and describe a favorite hobby or activity.

2. Tell children why you're here—to talk with them about what it means to be a Christian.

3. Encourage children to ask questions as often as they like. But don't be afraid to say, "I don't know" if you're not sure how to answer.

4. Begin by telling children what you learned last week (the basics of faith). Refer to your faith-sharing journal if necessary.

5. Tell children your own faith story.

6. Ask children what they don't understand about faith or Jesus (or what they'd like to know more about).

7. Explain how Christianity affects our daily choices (speak from your own experience).

8. Ask children about their fears or worries. Then see if you can apply your faith experience to those fears. For example, if someone tells you he or she is afraid of the dark, talk about how God is with us always, even when it's dark, and that we can talk to God when we're scared.

9. Allow children to talk about their own faith. Then close in prayer, thanking God for the opportunity to talk with them and learn more about what it means to them to be a Christian.

A few discussion tips:
- Spend as much time listening as talking.
- Be sincere.
- Expect surprising questions or answers.
- Don't judge kids' responses.
- Smile.

Permission to photocopy this handout granted for local church use. Copyright © Group Publishing, Inc., Box 481, Loveland, CO 80539.

OUR COMMITMENT—WEEK TWO

Use one or two of the ideas listed below to further explore the importance of talking about faith in clear language. Call your partner during the week to keep each other accountable to the task you've chosen. We'll discuss this experience next week.

Commitment Ideas:

❑ Talk with a pastor about the most effective ways to tell someone about Jesus.

❑ Together write a poem in word pictures that expresses your faith experience.

❑ Interview current or former missionaries about their experiences taking the gospel message to a foreign culture.

❑ Use simple craft supplies to create a visual symbol of what it means to be a Christian (and bring it to class next time).

❑ Find two or three Christian songs that describe one aspect of the Christian faith and discuss them. (Bring your favorite on tape to class next time, if possible.)

We, the undersigned, do hereby commit to follow through on the commitment plan checkmarked above.

Name_____Phone _____

Name_____Phone _____

Permission to photocopy this handout granted for local church use. Copyright © Group Publishing, Inc., Box 481, Loveland, CO 80539.

Everyday Faith

LESSON 3

One of the strongest statements we can make about our faith is the way we live our lives. This lesson will help teenagers discover the powerful witness their lives can be for the people around them.

Teenagers will discover the powerful witness of living out their faith in everyday situations.

Students will
- learn the importance of living out their faith,
- discover what it's like to be a living example of Christ,
- show love for people in the church or the surrounding community, and
- make a commitment to live out their faith in everyday situations.

Look up the following key Bible passages. Then read the background paragraphs to see how the passages relate to your teenagers. These Scripture passages will be explored during the Bible study portion of today's lesson.

In **1 Timothy 4:6-16**, Paul encourages Timothy to live an exemplary life.

In this passage, Paul points out the importance of setting an example for others in word, deed, and love. This passage teaches that Christians should pursue a consistent pattern in our faith lives.

As teenagers explore the prospect of sharing their faith, they may fail to consider how everyday actions affect their witness. This passage is a strong reminder that following Jesus in our words, actions, and love can positively influence the people we interact with.

In **Titus 2:1-8**, Paul describes a minister's duties.

This passage is clearly directed at the leaders and ministers of Paul's time. It deals specifically with the responsibilities Paul believes are required of church leaders.

Much of what Paul describes here is also valid for Christians who don't carry the title of "pastor" or "minister." The key to this passage is Paul's reminder to the leaders that they're to set a good example for those who are young in the faith. This same good

LESSON AIM

OBJECTIVES

BIBLE BASIS
1 TIMOTHY 4:6-16
TITUS 2:1-8

example is important for all Christians who are in a position to influence others.

Teenagers who want to share their faith with friends are going to be looked upon with great interest by those who don't agree with their Christian beliefs. Many will look upon their beliefs and laugh, while others will try to point out their faults to discredit Christianity. So it's essential that teenagers strive for the same kind of consistency Paul writes about in this passage. Not only does this consistency build a faith of great integrity, it also attracts others to find out more about what it means to be a Christian.

THIS LESSON AT A GLANCE

Section	Minutes	What Students Will Do	Supplies
Introduction	up to 10	**Action!**—Review their commitment activities and talk about the kind of movie they'd like to act in.	"Our Commitment— Week Two" handouts (p. 26) from last week
Bible Study	up to 10	**Just Live It**—Explore Bible passages that describe the importance of being good examples.	Bibles
Project Work	up to 35	**Let Your Actions Do the Talking**—Choose and perform activities that express their faith.	"Action Plans" handouts (p. 32)
	up to 10	**Commitment**—Determine how they'll live out their faith in the coming week.	"Our Commitment— Week Three" handouts (p. 33), pencils
Closing	up to 5	**By Our Love**—Sing a song and affirm each other's Christian example of love.	Songbooks

The Lesson

INTRODUCTION

Action!

(up to 10 minutes)

Welcome students to the class. Say: **Today, in our third week of this course on sharing your faith, we're going to explore the powerful witness of living out our faith in everyday life.**

Open with prayer.

Welcome visitors and class members who weren't here last week. Have a volunteer explain what the class is up to during this course.

Say: **Before we begin today's class, let's have commitment**

28 ■ LESSON THREE

pairs share insights from their activities during the past week.

Have kids find their partners from last week's "Commitment" activity. Distribute photocopies of the "Our Commitment—Week Two" handouts (p. 26) kids filled in last week. Have volunteers tell the whole class what they learned from their experiences. Encourage volunteers to share what was easy or difficult about following through with their commitments.

Thank kids for following through with their commitments.

Say: **Before we dive into today's Bible study, let's spend a couple of minutes discovering more about each other.**

Form trios. Have kids each answer the following question in their trios: **If you could act in any kind of movie, what kind would you choose and why? For example, you might say, "I'd be in an action film because I like to drive fast."**

Allow a few minutes for discussion, then say: **Today, we're going to explore how the way we act in real life can express our faith to others.**

Have kids who chose similar movie styles form groups of no more than four for the "Just Live It" activity.

Just Live It
(up to 10 minutes)

Assign each group one of the following passages: 1 Timothy 4:6-16 or Titus 2:1-8.

Say: **In your group, read the passage, then discuss how this passage's message can apply to your daily life.**

While groups are beginning to read the passage, go up to one group and instruct group members to behave badly while doing their reading and discussion. Encourage them to speak loudly, to goof off, and to try to annoy the other groups.

Allow no more than five minutes for reading and discussion. Then let kids in on the instructions you gave to the annoying group.

Ask:
- **How did it feel to be bothered by another group?** (Embarrassing; frustrating; annoying.)
- **If this were the kind of behavior non-Christians observed in Christian friends, what might they think of Christianity or these Christians?** (That Christianity is for hypocrites; that these people aren't really Christians; they'd be confused.)
- **How do our actions reflect who we are?** (If we act kindly toward others, we're probably kind people; people who don't care about others act with anger or violence toward people.)

Have volunteers each summarize their group's passage and determine what it means for us today.

Ask:
- **How is Paul's advice about being good examples valuable for us today?** (If we're good examples, others will want to know more about Christianity; if we act badly, we'll lose our integrity among non-Christians.)
- **How do our examples of faith help others discover what**

Teacher Tip

In the event that some pairs didn't do their work during the week, ask what kept them from completing the task. For example, kids may say that busyness or an unexpected event caused them to not do their task. Without placing blame or judgment on those pairs, ask, "How is your situation like what happens in real life when we try to share our faith? How can we keep 'urgent' or 'pressing' things from squeezing out 'important' things like sharing our faith with others?"

BIBLE STUDY

PROJECT WORK

it means to be a Christian? (By seeing how we show love, they learn how Jesus loves everyone; by recognizing our selfless attitudes, they learn that Christians are servants.)

Say: **Today, we're going to act on our faith and explore how our actions can help others discover God's love.**

Let Your Actions Do the Talking
(up to 35 minutes)

Have kids form trios. Then distribute photocopies of the "Action Plans" handout (p. 32) to each person.

Say: **For the next 20 to 30 minutes, you can perform any of the actions listed on this handout or make up your own. Choose only actions that you'll do sincerely and out of love. During this time, your goal is to express some aspect of your Christian faith to others. For example, cleaning a dirty floor would express a servant's attitude. Or visiting with an elderly church member or church neighbor might express patience and love.**

Help trios obtain any supplies they need for their activities, then send them on their way. Be sure to let students know when to return to the meeting room. You'll need about 15 minutes for the remaining class activities.

When trios return, assign each person in the trio a number from one to three. Then ask the following questions and call out a number from one to three. Ask the people with that number to briefly answer the question. Vary the numbers you call out so each person gets a chance to talk.

Ask:
- What did you enjoy most about your experience?
- How did you see the Christian faith acted out in each other's words and actions?
- Based on your experience, how can our actions shout God's love to others?
- How can we show God's love through our everyday lives?

Have kids discuss in their trios how being an example through actions and words is a way of sharing faith. Then have kids write their insights from today's lesson and experience in their faith-sharing journals. Have kids answer the following question in their journals:
- How can the example of our lives help others discover what it means to be a Christian?

Encourage kids to be specific as they list the things they can do to help others see God's love.

Commitment
(up to 10 minutes)

Have kids choose different commitment partners for this week's "Commitment" activity. Then distribute the "Our Commitment—Week Three" handout (p. 33) and a pencil to each pair.

Have pairs read and complete the commitment handouts.

Say: **Next week, we'll begin the class by reporting how our commitment plans worked and what we learned from them. Then we'll combine all we've explored in this course to create a visual reminder of what it means to share our faith with others. We'll present the finished product to the church as a reminder to all church members that we're to share our faith with the world.**

By Our Love
(up to 5 minutes)

CLOSING

Have kids form pairs. Say: **Today we've experienced just a sample of what it means to be good examples of Christ. As we go from here, we'll face many difficult times that may cause us to forget Paul's advice to be consistent in action and word. But with each other's prayers and support, we can be lights in the middle of a dark world.**

Have teenagers take a moment to say one thing they appreciate about their partners' Christian example in the world. For example, someone might say, "I appreciate how you're able to talk about faith boldly at school" or "I appreciate your willingness to serve others." Kids might mention something positive they saw their partners doing during today's lesson.

After kids have encouraged each other, close the lesson by singing "They Will Know We Are Christians By Our Love."

After the song, remind students to follow through on their commitment plans in the coming week. Encourage kids to take their journals home and record any insights from their experiences.

If You Still Have Time...

Serving Hearts—Form groups of no more than four and have groups choose one act of service they can perform for another group during the available time. Then have groups serve one another. Afterward, discuss how being a servant is a good way to share God's love with others.

Great Examples—Have kids brainstorm the names of Christians who've lived exemplary lives—either from the Bible or from more recent times. Then have teenagers determine what characteristics made these people great. Encourage students to develop these characteristics in their own lives.

ACTION PLANS

Use these ideas (or come up with your own) to practice living out your faith. In all these activities, be sincere in your attempt to be a good example for Christ.

Idea #1:

Visit a children's class and offer to help the teacher or teachers in any way.

Idea #2:

Visit people in the neighborhood and offer to help them with simple chores. Be sure to let people know you're from the church—but don't be surprised if people don't want your help.

Idea #3:

Find a dirty floor or hallway in the church and make it spotless. Check with your teacher to find cleaning supplies.

Idea #4:

Go around and warmly greet people who aren't in another class.

Idea #5:

Find someone in the church you can talk with about living out Christian faith (a pastor, church leader, or other mature Christian). Ask that person how our lives can be examples for Jesus. Listen carefully to the person's ideas and record his or her insights in your faith-sharing journals.

Idea #6:

Visit the church nursery and help take care of the infants. If the opportunity arises, change diapers, feed babies, or comfort them when they cry.

Idea #7:

Go around the church building and clean up any trash you find. If you run into people on the sidewalks, greet them with a smile.

Idea #8:

If your church is near a retirement community or shut-ins' homes, visit one or more of these people and spend a short time talking with them. Practice your listening skills and your patience at the same time.

Permission to photocopy this handout granted for local church use. Copyright © Group Publishing, Inc., Box 481, Loveland, CO 80539.

OUR COMMITMENT—WEEK THREE

Use one of the ideas listed below to further explore what it means to live out your faith. Call your partner during the week to keep each other accountable to the task you've chosen. We'll discuss this experience next week.

Commitment Ideas:

❏ Visit a nursing home and offer your help to the staff there. Or visit shut-ins and spend time talking with them.

❏ Choose someone you want to encourage (a friend or family member) and do nice things for that person. For example, you might write notes of encouragement, give the person a small gift, or offer to help out with a task. Don't ask for or expect anything in return.

❏ Give up an activity you really enjoy to do something helpful for a person at school. For example, instead of seeing a movie, help a school friend with homework.

❏ Read the book of Ephesians and write down all the advice Paul gives about how Christians should live their lives. Then discuss with a friend how well you follow this advice and how you can improve in your example of faith.

We, the undersigned, do hereby commit to follow through on the commitment plan checkmarked above.

Name_____Phone _____

Name_____Phone _____

LESSON 4

Putting the Pieces Together

In this course, teenagers have explored what it means to be a Christian and how to share their faith with others. To cap off the course, students will piece together all they've learned and create a lasting symbol of their faith-sharing experience.

LESSON AIM

Teenagers will create a mobile illustrating what they've learned about sharing their faith.

OBJECTIVES

Students will
- examine Jesus' great commission,
- form work teams and create a mobile depicting their course discoveries,
- affirm each other's role in the course, and
- commit to share their faith with others.

BIBLE BASIS

MATTHEW 28:18-20

Look up the following key Bible passage. Then read the background paragraphs to see how the passage relates to your teenagers. This Scripture will be explored during the Bible study portion of today's lesson.

In **Matthew 28:18-20**, Jesus commands his disciples to make disciples of all nations.

This passage, often referred to as the "great commission," is what guides us toward sharing our faith with others. But Jesus doesn't stop his message after asking us to share the good news. He also commands us to teach others how to live, beyond their first expression of faith in God.

This is an important message for teenagers who are eager to share the gospel message. They need to be available to their friends who *do* choose to follow Christ, to help them grow in faith.

34 ■ LESSON FOUR

THIS LESSON AT A GLANCE

Section	Minutes	What Students Will Do	Supplies
Introduction	up to 10	**Good Words**—Talk about how they've encouraged each other.	"Our Commitment—Week Three" handouts (p. 33) from last week, fruit
Bible Study	up to 10	**Go and Do**—Determine the twofold goal of Christ's great commission.	Bibles
Project Work	up to 35	**A Faith-Sharing Symbol**—Create a physical symbol of their faith-sharing insights.	Sturdy hook, large sheets of Foamcore or heavy cardboard, strong cord or string, markers, utility knives, wooden dowels, "Mobile Ideas" handouts (p. 40)
	up to 10	**Wrap-Up and Review**—Review the past weeks' lessons and determine what they enjoyed most about the course.	
Closing	up to 10	**Let the Sharing Begin**—Dedicate the faith-sharing symbol and present it to the church.	"Dedication Ceremony" handouts (p. 41)

The Lesson

Good Words
(up to 10 minutes)

Welcome students to the class. Say: **Today, in our final week of this course on sharing our faith, we're going to combine all we've learned and create a lasting faith-sharing symbol and present it to the whole church.**

Open with prayer.

Welcome visitors and class members who weren't here last week. Have a volunteer explain what the class is up to during this course.

Say: **Before we begin today's class, let's have commitment pairs share insights from their activities during the past week.**

Have kids find their partners from last week's "Commitment" activity. Distribute photocopies of the "Our Commitment—Week Three" handouts (p. 33) kids filled in last week. Have volunteers tell the whole class what they learned from their experiences. Encourage volunteers to share what was easy or difficult about following through with their commitments.

INTRODUCTION

Teacher Tip

In the event that some pairs didn't do their work during the week, ask what kept them from completing the task. For example, kids may say that busyness or an unexpected event caused them to not do their task. Without placing blame or judgment on those pairs, ask, "How is your situation like what happens in real life when we try to share our faith? How can we keep 'urgent' or 'pressing' things from squeezing out 'important' things like sharing our faith with others?"

BIBLE STUDY

Thank kids for following through with their commitments.

Say: **Each week we've spent a little time getting to know each other better. This week we'll take that time to thank each other for specific things we've appreciated during the past weeks.**

Form groups of no more than four. Have kids choose the people they've worked with the most to be in their group. Form a special group for guests or visitors to today's class. Give kids each a piece of fruit.

Say: **Think about the people in your group and how they've helped you enjoy the past three weeks on sharing your faith. Then, beginning with the person who looks most like me, tell how someone in your group has encouraged you or inspired you these past few weeks. For example, you might say, "This person has inspired me by being open to new ideas." Then hand your fruit to that person. Then that person says something about another person in your group. Continue until each person has been affirmed and each person has a piece of fruit.**

Since the visitors won't have built relationships in class, have the people in your group tell about a person they've been inspired by in their faith lives, then hand the fruit to someone else. Or, visitors can join in groups with someone who knows them.

When groups are finished, say: **We've learned a lot about each other, as well as how we can share our faith with others. As we enjoy eating our fruit, let's remember that the goal of sharing faith is to bear fruit and bring others into the family of God.**

Have teenagers enjoy their fruit while you move on to the next activity.

Go and Do
(up to 10 minutes)

Form pairs. Quietly tell one person in each pair to turn to Matthew 28:18-20 and read it silently. Don't let the other students know which passage their partners are reading. Then have the readers attempt to illustrate the message of the passage through actions (but no words). See how accurately the other partners can guess the message of the Scripture passage.

After a few minutes, get students' attention and ask the following questions:

■ **How did those of you who were reading the passage feel about trying to act out the message?** (Embarrassed; stifled; uncomfortable.)

■ **What was it like for those of you who were trying to guess the message of the passage?** (Frustrating; fun; confusing.)

■ **What does this experience tell us about the value of our words and actions in communication?** (What we say matters; it takes both actions and words to communicate things.)

■ **How can we use what we've learned in the past three weeks to better share our faith in action and words?** (Answers will vary.)

Have a volunteer read aloud Matthew 28:18-20 for the whole class. Then ask:
- **What are the implications of this passage for Christians today?** (We must tell others about Christ; we're to teach others how to follow Jesus.)
- **What are our responsibilities to those who choose to follow Christ?** (To teach them; to guide them in their daily walk; to help them know what's right and wrong.)

Say: **When we share our faith with others, we're taking the first step of obedience to Jesus' command in Matthew 28:18-20. But the second step, teaching people about the Christian lifestyle, is just as important.**

A Faith-Sharing Symbol
(up to 35 minutes)

PROJECT WORK

During the next 25 to 35 minutes, your students will create a large, hanging mobile to symbolize sharing faith. Get permission from your pastor or your church's building committee to hang the finished mobile in a prominent place in your church. When the mobile is finished, ask your pastor to join your class in dedicating the symbol.

Put a sturdy hook into the ceiling where you'll hang the mobile. You may want your mobile to hang above the church members' heads or hang in a corner of the foyer from the ceiling to the floor. After you've chosen your location, measure to determine the maximum length and width for the finished mobile. You'll need these measurements when you assemble the mobile.

Form three groups. If your class is larger than 12, form six or nine groups of no more than four. Assign each group one of the following three topics: "Know the basics," "Speak simply and from experience," and "Let your faith shine through your actions."

Set out a large supply of Foamcore (available in multiple colors through art-supply stores), strong cord or string, markers, utility knives, and wooden dowels. Groups will each need at least one large sheet of Foamcore and a utility knife. If you can't get Foamcore, choose heavy cardboard instead (although Foamcore is preferred because it's easy to cut and is lighter than strong cardboard).

Say: **We're going to create a huge mobile to symbolize the various aspects of sharing your faith. Each of your topics is a summary of one of our three previous lessons. Using the supplies in the room, create a portion of this mobile that depicts your topic.**

You may cut your Foamcore into various shapes, write words or draw pictures on the Foamcore, and piece shapes together to form three-dimensional objects to be attached to our mobile. Then attach string to the pieces so they can be hung from each other or from the wooden dowels.

You'll have about 20 minutes to prepare your mobile sections. Then we'll work together to create the finished product.

Teacher Tip

To avoid the risk of scratching tables or cutting the carpet, have a sheet of plywood available for kids to use as a cutting board when cutting the Foamcore with the utility knives.

CLOSING

Have kids refer to their faith-sharing journals for notes and insights on what to include in their mobile sections.

Use the "Mobile Ideas" handout (p. 40) to give kids ideas on what they might include in their mobiles. Also, have one group create a "header" or title piece for the mobile with the words "Sharing Your Faith Without Fear" written on both sides. Place this header at the top or bottom of the mobile in a prominent place.

When kids have finished preparing their mobile sections, have them briefly describe what they created and why. Then have kids work together to tie mobile sections together and to the wooden dowels to create the final mobile. Remind kids to balance elements on the dowels so the dowels remain horizontal. Refer to the measurements you took earlier to make sure the mobile will fit where it's going to be placed.

When the mobile is finished, have kids each pick up a piece and carry it together to the place where it will hang. Have kids hang the mobile and adjust mobile pieces on the wooden dowels as necessary to balance the mobile. Then have kids sit for a brief review of the course before closing today's lesson with a dedication of the mobile.

Wrap-Up and Review
(up to 10 minutes)

Form groups of no more than four and have kids answer the following questions in their groups:
- **What has impacted you most about this course?**
- **What memory from this course will stay with you for a long time?**
- **What's one positive thing that happened in your life as a result of this course?**
- **What have you learned about sharing your faith that you can use in your daily life?**

When kids have finished discussing the questions, have volunteers tell the whole group how the course has impacted them in their daily lives. Thank kids for their honest responses.

Let the Sharing Begin
(up to 10 minutes)

Invite your pastor to join your group for the dedication of your faith-sharing mobile. Use the ceremony on the "Dedication Ceremony" handout (p. 41) or create your own.

After the ceremony, have students go around and thank each other for their good insights and hard work in the past four weeks. Then form a large circle (around or under the mobile, if possible) and have each person complete the following one-sentence commitment: **One thing I'm going to do to share my faith with others is...**

Close with a big group hug and a hearty "amen."

Ask teenagers to stay near the mobile to answer questions for congregation members who are just arriving for worship or are heading home after the education hour. Ask the pastor to make an announcement about the mobile during worship and allow volunteers from your class to briefly explain what it means. (Have the volunteers refer to the "Dedication Ceremony" handout for ideas on what to say.)

Keep the mobile hanging as long as possible to remind all church members about the importance of sharing our faith. Encourage kids to use their faith-sharing journals to record future insights about what it means to fulfill our Lord's command to make disciples of all the nations.

If You Still Have Time...

Faith Reminders—Have kids create small faith reminders out of the Foamcore scraps to take home or give away. For example, kids might cut out cross-shaped pieces and write "Share the News" on them.

MOBILE IDEAS

Here are a few starter ideas for creating your mobile. Use these or create your own.

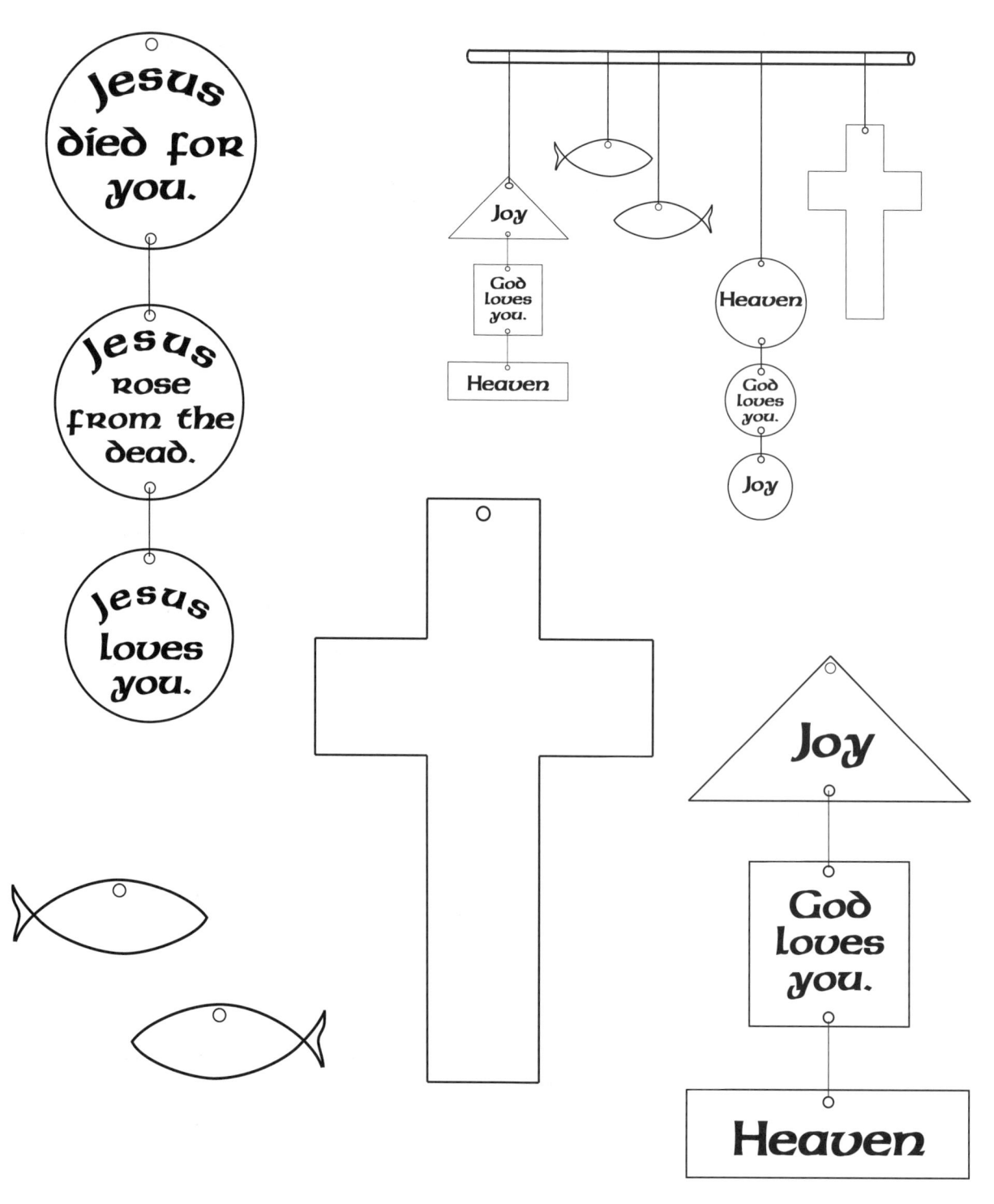

Permission to photocopy this handout granted for local church use. Copyright © Group Publishing, Inc., Box 481, Loveland, CO 80539.

DEDICATION CEREMONY

Use this simple ceremony to dedicate your faith-sharing mobile.

Have everyone stand facing the mobile.

Pastor: As we dedicate this symbol of sharing our faith, let's not focus on the cardboard and markers that make up this mobile, but on the hearts and minds of the people who created it.
Dear God, we dedicate this mobile as a symbol of all Christians who desire to share your good news...

People: ...with our friends, our families, and all the nations.

Pastor: As this mobile is guided by the wind...

People: ...may we be guided by the Holy Spirit.

Pastor: Give us the words to speak...

People: ...and the confidence to speak them.

Pastor: Help us to follow in Jesus' footsteps...

People: ...and be powerful examples of Christian faith.

All: Guide and direct us as we strive to fulfill your great commission—to preach Christ to the nations. Amen.

Have everyone put the mobile in motion by gently blowing on it or fanning it in unison.

As people watch the mobile in motion, have them silently ask God for the strength and confidence to bring Christ's message to the nations.

Bonus Ideas

MEETINGS AND MORE

Bonus Scriptures—The lessons focus on a select few Scripture passages, but if you'd like to incorporate more Bible readings into a lesson, here are some suggestions:
- Acts 16:31 (Believe in Jesus and you will be saved.)
- Romans 6:23 (The gift of God is eternal life.)
- Romans 14:11 (Every knee will bow before God.)
- 1 Corinthians 10:27-29 (Don't let your freedom be judged by another's conscience.)
- Ephesians 2:8-9 (By grace we are saved, through faith.)
- 1 John 1:9 (If we confess our sins, God will forgive us.)
- 1 John 3:14-20 (We know we've passed from death to life if we love our brothers.)

Disciple Teams—Talk with your pastor to get the names of mature, adult Christians in your church. Then invite these adults each to match up with two or three interested teenagers for a weekly time of discipling by the adults. Have kids choose the issues they'd like to learn more about, especially relating to faith basics and sharing faith with others. Encourage adults to share their experiences in telling people about Jesus.

On the Street—Form groups of no more than three and have them determine a way to share the gospel message with people on the streets of your city or town. Encourage groups to come up with creative, but not manipulative, methods for talking with people or illustrating for others what it means to be a Christian.

Success Stories—Invite church members who've successfully shared their faith with others to come and speak to your young people. Encourage these adults to talk about the positive and negative aspects of their faith-sharing experiences.

Mini-Mission Trip—Work with a retired or furloughed missionary to develop a local mini-mission trip for teenagers. Have the missionary help develop a plan for spreading the good news about Jesus to people in your community (such as homeless people, children at a day-care center, or nursing home residents). Be sure to get permission for kids to talk about Jesus if you choose a nursing home, day-care center, or other institution that isn't specifically run by Christians.

Debrief the experience afterward and have the missionary speak about his or her experiences.

Continuing the Faith Journal—Have kids continue to keep track of everyday evangelism experiences in their faith-sharing journals from the course. Meet monthly with kids who continue to use these journals to discuss new entries and insights they have from their faith-sharing experiences.

Over the Airwaves—Have kids contact local radio stations and see if they can get air time for a weekly half-hour radio show on being a Christian in today's non-Christian world (or a similar topic). If necessary, have the church help by raising funds for the show.

For a radio show, kids could play Christian music and talk about what Christ means to them. Or they could have a call-in show for kids to ask questions about Christianity (have a pastor or counselor on hand for the tougher questions).

Music Swap—Take kids to your local Christian bookstore and have the store clerk help them choose Christian music that might appeal to their non-Christian friends. Ask your church's outreach committee to subsidize their purchases.

Then have kids give these tapes to non-Christian friends as a discussion starter about what it means to be a Christian.

PARTY PLEASERS

Games With a Message—Plan a games night for your kids that will include faith discussions relating to the games. For example, kids might use the game Hide-and-Seek as a lead-in to a discussion about when they feel like hiding their faith. Or, an uneven-team game of volleyball could springboard into a discussion of how the world may not always seem fair to Christians.

Feed Me, Then Feed Me Again—Have teenagers invite non-Christian friends to a pizza party at your church or a local pizza restaurant. Tell teenagers to let their friends know you'll be talking about faith during the eating time but that they'll at least get a free meal out of the deal.

During the party, have kids talk openly about their joys and struggles with their faith. Encourage non-Christians to join in the discussion and ask questions about what it means to be a Christian.

After the party, remind your young people that sometimes we don't see the results of our evangelistic efforts until much later—or not at all. Thank kids for their courage to bring non-Christian friends to the party and encourage them to reach out in love to those people during the week.

RETREAT IDEA

Tell Me More—Invite your pastor to lead a retreat designed to help teenagers explore what it means to be a Christian. Then have kids invite their non-Christian friends to the retreat to explore faith with them. Have kids let their friends know they won't be pressured to choose Christianity but that they'll be able to explore what it means through discussion, activities, and relationships.

Use a variety of activities from such creative resources as Group's Active Bible Curriculum™ titles *What's a Christian?* and *Who is Jesus?*

Expect a different "flavor" during this retreat as non-Christian kids and Christian kids interact about life. Plan plenty of fun activities and good food to help everyone see that faith can be fun.

At the end of the retreat (or any time during the retreat), offer to talk one to one with kids who are interested in becoming Christians.

CURRICULUM REORDER—TOP PRIORITY

Order now to prepare for your upcoming Sunday school classes, youth ministry meetings, and weekend retreats! Each book includes all teacher and student materials—plus photocopiable handouts—for any size class . . . for just $8.99 each!

FOR SENIOR HIGH:

- **1 & 2 Corinthians: Christian Discipleship,** ISBN 1-55945-230-7
- **Angels, Demons, Miracles & Prayer,** ISBN 1-55945-235-8
- **Changing the World,** ISBN 1-55945-236-6
- **Christians in a Non-Christian World,** ISBN 1-55945-224-2
- **Christlike Leadership,** ISBN 1-55945-231-5
- **Communicating With Friends,** ISBN 1-55945-228-5
- **Counterfeit Religions,** ISBN 1-55945-207-2
- **Dating Decisions,** ISBN 1-55945-215-3
- **Dealing With Life's Pressures,** ISBN 1-55945-232-3
- **Deciphering Jesus' Parables,** ISBN 1-55945-237-4
- **Exodus: Following God,** ISBN 1-55945-226-9
- **Exploring Ethical Issues,** ISBN 1-55945-225-0
- **Faith for Tough Times,** ISBN 1-55945-216-1
- **Forgiveness,** ISBN 1-55945-223-4
- **Getting Along With Parents,** ISBN 1-55945-202-1
- **Getting Along With Your Family,** ISBN 1-55945-233-1
- **The Gospel of John: Jesus' Teachings,** ISBN 1-55945-208-0
- **Hazardous to Your Health: AIDS, Steroids & Eating Disorders,** ISBN 1-55945-200-5
- **Is Marriage in Your Future?,** ISBN 1-55945-203-X
- **Jesus' Death & Resurrection,** ISBN 1-55945-211-0
- **The Joy of Serving,** ISBN 1-55945-210-2
- **Knowing God's Will,** ISBN 1-55945-205-6
- **Life After High School,** ISBN 1-55945-220-X
- **Making Good Decisions,** ISBN 1-55945-209-9
- **Money: A Christian Perspective,** ISBN 1-55945-212-9
- **Movies, Music, TV & Me,** ISBN 1-55945-213-7
- **Overcoming Insecurities,** ISBN 1-55945-221-8
- **Psalms,** ISBN 1-55945-234-X
- **Real People, Real Faith: Amy Grant, Joni Eareckson Tada, Dave Dravecky, Terry Anderson,** ISBN 1-55945-238-2
- **Responding to Injustice,** ISBN 1-55945-214-5
- **Revelation,** ISBN 1-55945-229-3
- **School Struggles,** ISBN 1-55945-201-3
- **Sex: A Christian Perspective,** ISBN 1-55945-206-4
- **Today's Lessons From Yesterday's Prophets,** ISBN 1-55945-227-7
- **Turning Depression Upside Down,** ISBN 1-55945-135-1
- **What Is the Church?,** ISBN 1-55945-222-6
- **Who Is God?,** ISBN 1-55945-218-8
- **Who Is Jesus?,** ISBN 1-55945-219-6
- **Who Is the Holy Spirit?,** ISBN 1-55945-217-X
- **Your Life as a Disciple,** ISBN 1-55945-204-8

FOR JUNIOR HIGH/MIDDLE SCHOOL:

- **Accepting Others: Beyond Barriers & Stereotypes,** ISBN 1-55945-126-2
- **Advice to Young Christians: Exploring Paul's Letters,** ISBN 1-55945-146-7
- **Applying the Bible to Life,** ISBN 1-55945-116-5
- **Becoming Responsible,** ISBN 1-55945-109-2
- **Bible Heroes: Joseph, Esther, Mary & Peter,** ISBN 1-55945-137-8
- **Boosting Self-Esteem,** ISBN 1-55945-100-9
- **Building Better Friendships,** ISBN 1-55945-138-6
- **Can Christians Have Fun?,** ISBN 1-55945-134-3
- **Caring for God's Creation,** ISBN 1-55945-121-1
- **Christmas: A Fresh Look,** ISBN 1-55945-124-6
- **Competition,** ISBN 1-55945-133-5
- **Dealing With Death,** ISBN 1-55945-112-2
- **Dealing With Disappointment,** ISBN 1-55945-139-4
- **Doing Your Best,** ISBN 1-55945-142-4
- **Drugs & Drinking,** ISBN 1-55945-118-1
- **Evil and the Occult,** ISBN 1-55945-102-5
- **Genesis: The Beginnings,** ISBN 1-55945-111-4
- **Guys & Girls: Understanding Each Other,** ISBN 1-55945-110-6
- **Handling Conflict,** ISBN 1-55945-125-4
- **Heaven & Hell,** ISBN 1-55945-131-9
- **Is God Unfair?,** ISBN 1-55945-108-4
- **Love or Infatuation?,** ISBN 1-55945-128-9
- **Making Parents Proud,** ISBN 1-55945-107-6
- **Making the Most of School,** ISBN 1-55945-113-0
- **Materialism,** ISBN 1-55945-130-0
- **The Miracle of Easter,** ISBN 1-55945-143-2
- **Miracles!,** ISBN 1-55945-117-3
- **Peace & War,** ISBN 1-55945-123-8
- **Peer Pressure,** ISBN 1-55945-103-3
- **Prayer,** ISBN 1-55945-104-1
- **Reaching Out to a Hurting World,** ISBN 1-55945-140-8
- **Sermon on the Mount,** ISBN 1-55945-129-7
- **Suicide: The Silent Epidemic,** ISBN 1-55945-145-9
- **Telling Your Friends About Christ,** ISBN 1-55945-114-9
- **The Ten Commandments,** ISBN 1-55945-127-0
- **Today's Faith Heroes: Madeline Manning Mims, Michael W. Smith, Mother Teresa, Bruce Olson,** ISBN 1-55945-141-6
- **Today's Media: Choosing Wisely,** ISBN 1-55945-144-0
- **Today's Music: Good or Bad?,** ISBN 1-55945-101-7
- **What Is God's Purpose for Me?,** ISBN 1-55945-132-7
- **What's a Christian?,** ISBN 1-55945-105-X

Order today from your local Christian bookstore, or write: Group Publishing, Box 485, Loveland, CO 80539. For mail orders, please add postage/handling of $4 for orders up to $15, $5 for orders of $15.01+. Colorado residents add 3% sales tax.

MORE PROGRAMMING IDEAS FOR YOUR ACTIVE GROUP...

DO IT! ACTIVE LEARNING IN YOUTH MINISTRY
Thom and Joani Schultz

Discover the keys to teaching creative faith-building lessons that teenagers look forward to…and remember for a lifetime. You'll learn how to design simple, fun programs that will help your kids…

- build community,
- develop communication skills,
- relate better to others,
- experience what it's really like to be a Christian,

…and apply the Bible to their daily challenges. Plus, you'll get 24 ready-to-use active-learning exercises complete with debriefing questions and Bible application. For example, your kids will…

- learn the importance of teamwork and the value of each team member by juggling six different objects as a group,
- experience community and God's grace using a doughnut,
- grow more sensitive to others' needs by acting out Matthew 25:31-46

…just to name a few. And the practical index of over 30 active-learning resources will make your planning easier.

ISBN 0-931529-94-8

DEVOTIONS FOR YOUTH GROUPS ON THE GO
Dan and Cindy Hansen

Now it's easy to turn every youth group trip into an opportunity for spiritual growth for your kids. This resource gives you 52 easy-to-prepare devotions that teach meaningful spiritual lessons using the experiences of your group's favorite outings. You'll get devotions perfect for everything from amusement parks, to choir trips, to miniature golf, to the zoo. Your kids will gain new insights from the Bible as they…

- discuss how many "strikes" God gives us—after enjoying a game of softball,
- experience the hardship of Jesus' temptation in the wilderness—on a camping trip,
- understand the disciples' relief when Jesus calmed the storm—while white-water rafting, even

…learn to trust God's will when bad weather cancels an event or the bus breaks down! Plus, the handy topical listing makes your planning easy.

ISBN 1-55945-075-4

Order today from your local Christian bookstore, or write: Group Publishing, Box 485, Loveland, CO 80539. For mail orders, please add postage/handling of $4 for orders up to $15, $5 for orders of $15.01+. Colorado residents add 3% sales tax.

PUT FAITH INTO ACTION WITH...

Want to try something different with your 7th—12th grade classes? Group's NEW Projects With a Purpose™ for Youth Ministry offers four-week courses that really get kids into their faith. Each Project With a Purpose course gives you tools to facilitate a project that will provide a direct, purposeful learning experience. Teenagers will discover something significant about their faith while learning the importance of working together, sharing one another's troubles, and supporting one another in love…plus they'll have lots of fun!

Each lesson-complete leaders book offers four sessions. Use for Sunday school classes, midweek, home Bible studies, youth groups, retreats, or any time you want to help teenagers discover more about their faith.

These easy-to-teach lessons will help your teenagers learn deep insights about their faith! Your kids will learn more about each other. They'll practice the life skill of working together. And you'll be rewarded with the knowledge that you're providing a life-changing, faith-building experience for your church's teenagers.

Titles Available:

Acting Out Jesus' Parables	1-55945-147-5
Celebrating Christ With Youth-Led Worship	1-55945-410-5
Checking Your Church's Pulse	1-55945-408-3
Serving Your Neighbors	1-55945-406-7
Teaching Teenagers to Pray	1-55945-407-5
Teenagers Teaching Children	1-55945-405-9
Videotaping Your Church Members' Faith Stories	1-55945-239-0

Order today from your local Christian bookstore, or write: Group Publishing, Box 485, Loveland, CO 80539. For mail orders, please add postage/handling of $4 for orders up to $15, $5 for orders of $15.01+. Colorado residents add 3% sales tax.